THE EFFECT OF YOUR LIFE OR YOUR MONEY

THE POWER OF FINANCIAL INDEPENDENCE TRANSFORM LIVES

JOHN S. MCDONALD

Copyright©2023 John S. McDonald

All Rights Reserved

TABLE OF CONTENT

INTRODUCTION

CHAPTER ONE
    With mindfulness, we can put this into practice!

CHAPTER TWO
    7 Steps to Decluttering Your Life Pin for Pinterest

CHAPTER THREE
    how-to-build-wealth

CHAPTER FOUR
    Methods for Saving Money and the Environment

INTRODUCTION

Having enough money or assets to cover one's living needs for the rest of one's life without having to work or rely on others is the state of being financially independent. [1] Passive income is a term used to describe revenue obtained without the need of doing a job. [Reference required] Depending on their objectives, others may define financial independence in various ways.

There are several ways to become financially independent, and each has advantages and disadvantages. A financial plan and budget may be useful for someone who wants to become financially independent because it gives them a clear picture of their existing revenues and spending and enables them to identify and choose the best ways to reach their financial objectives. Every facet of a person's financial situation is covered by a financial plan. searching all day for someone who desires it—looking for someone who understands how to look after, develop, and expand it.

This is so that people may understand how money works. There must aways be a transmission of an electric current. It will perish if it is unable to find a new home. Money is called currency for this reason. Otherwise, it will likewise perish, thus it must move someplace. Savers are losers for this reason. Savings eventually lose value due to inflation. Money must move to places where it may expand to stay alive. People with strong financial intelligence can discern where money is moving and how to follow it.

Money will come to you and be thrown at you if you know how to handle it, particularly in trying times. Many will urge you to accept it. Money won't come your way if you don't know how to handle it.

The truth is that if you possess a high level of financial intelligence, you can identify areas where money is moving, arrive there ahead of others, benefit from that money by acquiring assets that appreciate and generate income, and then use that money to buy more assets where additional money is moving. Money works for you when you put in the effort to see. It's not a magic trick, but to be successful at it, you need to study like one. The finest thing you could do with your time to improve is devoted years of attention to it.

CHAPTER ONE

With mindfulness, we can put this into practice!

When you're shopping and an urge strikes, pause to take a few deep breaths and deal with the issue thoughtfully. Think about it:
What feelings am I experiencing at the moment?
Is there a reason for these feelings?
What other options do I have besides buying this thing to deal with these feelings?
We aren't identifying or condemning any feelings that come to mind, just as in mindful meditation. Instead, we are only acknowledging their presence. I spent five minutes taking deep breaths and meditating as I stared at a pint of ice cream in the

freezer area. Did I come across as a bit odd? Indeed, I did! Did I purchase the ice cream on a whim? Though difficult, I did not give up.

Be aware of your requirements and consider your goals.

If everything were clear-cut, we would only purchase what we need. Being able to avoid spending money on unnecessary demands is crucial when money is limited. However, a lot of those desires are for things that, at the time, make us happy or reduce our tension. That's rather good! However, it's crucial to consider which desires are most crucial as well as the potential effects of spending any more funds.

Making a "mindful wishes wishlist" of items you know you don't need but would make you happy or benefit another aspect of your well-being may be helpful.

Spend some time with each thing and give serious consideration to why it made the list.

- I want to purchase this, but why?
- What about this would be enjoyable for me?
- Will it lessen the stress I'm under?
- How long will I feel this way after I buy something?
- Can I have this sensation without spending this money in another way?
- We may pick the desires that will benefit us the most and that have the most worth by reflecting on issues like these.
- Why mindfulness is important

As I alluded to before, mindfulness may be helpful in many aspects of our everyday life. Impulsive purchases could decline as stress decreases. Making better decisions may assist us in making those difficult decisions while creating or maintaining a budget. Our ability to do our jobs better might result in overall financial gains!

Try using mindfulness techniques in other aspects of your life if you have any positive effects from any of these mindful money activities (or even if you don't). It's crucial to keep in mind that mindfulness-based financial practices are not a quick panacea for all of your financial difficulties.

Instead, mindful money practices help us make choices that are more in line with our values and financial objectives by using mindfulness skills.

CHAPTER TWO

7 Steps to Decluttering Your Life Pin for Pinterest

It probably won't come as a surprise to you if you're reading this because a life full of clutter also means a life full of stress. You can never locate what you need when you need it, which results in frantic morning searches and additional mess-cleaning tasks at night. We generally feel out of control when our environment is unmanageable. Additionally, clutter has a peculiar way of finding its way into every aspect of life—at home, at work, in the automobile, and everywhere else!

However, decluttering your life entails more than just cleaning and arranging your physical environment. It necessitates carefully planning your time and setting priorities for your duties.

Fortunately, it is possible to feel uncluttered again when you divide the decluttering procedure into portions and develop game plans for each aspect of your life.

We're examining all the areas in life where clutter may quickly accumulate, including:

- Your habits and thinking
- Your timetable
- The house's Online existence
- Paper records
- at work driving

After going through each of these topics, we hope you can come up with a game plan of your own and begin working toward your goal of a decluttered existence. Links to other articles have been supplied along the way for those who want to learn more about almost every topic. Continue reading to discover how to finally simplify your life.

Prepare yourself mentally to organize your life.

When you organize your life, you free up your thinking.

If you're serious about decluttering, you should begin by looking inward at your actions and habits. What bad behaviors have you developed that is the root of the clutter? Are you neglecting a few urgent tasks? Are your organization's needs reasonable given your schedule and the responsibilities of daily life? You may start fixing some of your fundamental clutter-causing issues only once you have a better understanding of them.

Be honest with yourself about why you want to purge your space of clutter. When you feel unmotivated, remember why you do what you do. Would you like to create a room in your house for a hobby? Are you selling your surplus to earn some more money? Maintaining your attention on your objective will serve as a constant reminder that clearing away the clutter will be worthwhile. As you attempt to simplify your life, think about writing out your objective and posting it somewhere visible in your house.

Start thinking about how you may simplify your life in addition to assessing your habits and concentrating on your objective. Maybe now is the moment to do less and have less.

When you declutter, you don't only reorganize your tangible possessions. It may also imply that you are making all aspects of your life simpler. You may psychologically get ready for a true decluttering journey in the following ways:

Adopt some minimalist living principles. (Take some pointers on how to live minimally from an uncommitted minimalist me.)

Try freezing your screen. For one whole day each week, put your phone and applications away and rediscover your passion for reading, board games, or bike trips.

Free yourself from the relentless desire of contemporary society to be informed at all times by turning off the TV or the news.

Make a conscious effort to limit your overall screen time.

Spend more time on yourself and learn to say "no" when necessary. Make time for the things that are most important to you by giving them top priority, and achieving them first.

To give yourself the mental space you need to make wise decluttering choices, practice mindfulness.

Sort through your schedule.

A calendar is a great tool for organizing your schedule and life.

Our busy schedules often encourage clutter. When we are overbooked, we move quickly from one location to the next, leaving little time to arrange things properly.

If you don't already, start doing so. If so, consider the week and month that are ahead. Start by listing all of the things that must be done. Then, give the remaining items on your list some serious thought. Are they worthwhile to retain in your calendar in terms of time and effort?

Weekly planning for yourself and your family is time well spent, so make a deliberate effort to do so. You may better prepare for forthcoming activities and prevent hectic mornings that often result in extra clutter by planning your week.

Laura provided a helpful six-step regimen for weekly life organization. Take a moment to read it!

Do you struggle to get your family members' calendars in sync? Try keeping a calendar in a prominent place where everyone can access it often and contribute to it. Perhaps this year will mark your transition to utilizing apps to manage your shared to-do lists.

Planning your meals might also help you "declutter" your calendar. Instead of purchasing a ton of stuff, you may cook later, you'll know exactly what to purchase from the grocery store if you plan your meals out weekly. You'll purchase fewer unnecessary items and create less waste overall if you plan and know what you need before you go shopping. At the end of the day, you won't have to worry about what to have for supper. Plan and prepare your meals in advance to keep yourself and your family well-fed and on task throughout a hectic week.

Plan your home so that it fits your schedule. Organize your life at home with some advice and a strategy.

Although there is more to decluttering than just the physical realm, your surroundings are a great place to start. Some people believe that clutter on the exterior also equals clutter within. So if you're attempting to declutter your life, organizing your house is a wonderful place to start.

The home organization might seem like a never-ending cycle, particularly when done in a communal setting. It's possible that what worked for your family last year or even season won't continue to work in the future. Your home organization must adapt to changes in your job, school, and everyday routines.

It could be a good idea to review your organization's approach when it's time to find a home for all of those brand-new Christmas presents and gadgets. Spend some time cleaning up the seasonal clothing clutter, reevaluating the guest bathroom storage options, and cleaning the kitchen and pantry after all the Christmas meals.

Closets are difficult to organize, so work on them when you're feeling most energized and motivated.

Check out my home organizing tour for the specifics on how to organize your house. It guides you through your home's issue areas and clutter hotspots room by room with particular information.

Organize your online presence.

How to Purge Your Digital Life of Clutter

When decluttering, you should give your digital life at least equal attention to that given to your physical surroundings. To put it mildly, the quantity of information that is offered to us when we pick up our phones or go on to the web is overwhelming. Monitoring the quantity of inputs we permit in our life is beneficial.

Giving yourself a blank slate in your email is an excellent approach to streamline your digital life. Keep the unnecessary information out of your inbox by unsubscribing from superfluous newsletters and advertising emails that don't add any value to your life. Create a new inbox if your current one is out of control. As chances arise, such as when there are payments that are overdue, you may establish up significant accounts under your new address one at a time.

Computer data may be quite daunting. To ensure that all of your memories are current and secure, it is crucial to create backup copies of your photos. But if you don't have any kind of system in place for organizing, your computer may become another another location where clutter creeps into our life.

Spend some time classifying documents by topic or chronological order. Create folders, then backup your data to external hard drives. Additionally, upload the data and photographs from your mobile phone to your hard disks or digital devices. Maintain a plan and regularly backup your data so you aren't depending on erratic PCs and mobile devices to maintain crucial media files. Losing digital material is upsetting. You avoid clogging up your computer once again, be sure to take the time to put everything in the appropriate folders.

To ensure that you never again have to spend time organizing digital data, make a commitment to maintain your new filing system going forward.

Organize your paper trail.

The most challenging aspect of cleaning your life is organizing your documents.

One of the best ways to simplify your life is to organize and save your vital paperwork. It's crucial to make an investment in a filing system that can protect your confidential data. Finding a way to keep all of your correspondence and daily paperwork organized is as important, however.

The time is here for your message center to install a mail sorting station. How are you going to organize all the school documents, invoices, and flyers that are sent every day? Making it a routine to file your paperwork each day can help you keep the process under control.

It is simple to get distracted by the memories in the middle of organizing while dealing with sensitive documents like cards and pictures. Many of us are prevented from taking action by this. However, there are excellent methods for controlling these kinds of articles. Here are some creative methods to display emotional cards so that you may make use of them, along with our best advice for organizing photos.

Let the purging permeate your professional life.

Be clear about your priorities first. By establishing some balance in your life, you may begin organizing your workspace. Make sure your objectives are specific so you can decide how much time you want to devote to your work.

Next, make the appropriate adjustments to make the most of your time spent away from home. Perhaps automating one of your initiatives is necessary for that. Maybe people are starting to work from home more. Working from home has several advantages, including less commutes, more time with family, and a bit less stress, all of which contribute to a life that is uncluttered. You'll need a designated workplace in your home if you want to implement that plan without just adding more work clutter.

One apparent piece of advise is to clear your workplace, wherever you chose to work. A neat workstation encourages concentrated work, just as desiring a clean kitchen before you start cooking. Here is a useful starter guide from PopSugar.

Clean out your automobile as well.

How to simplify your life while also cleaning out your automobile

For the majority of us, the automobile resembles a mobile workplace. Random stuff accumulate in the cramped area of your vehicle since you're always on the move, picking up family members, and waiting for the next opportunity to rush kids off to school or one of their numerous activities.

Since it needs to be cleaned often as a result, keeping it tidy will also help maintain it clutter-free.

At the absolute least, provide room for random essentials like Kleenex by adding storage to seat backs and pockets. Of course, you should also have a place to put rubbish.

Last but not least, agree as a family that whatever you carry into the vehicle will go with you. As a result, there shouldn't be as many heaps of shoes, water bottles, and toys to remove from the family car each week.

For a new start, decluttering physically may be sufficient in certain cases, but other times you need to do more than simply purge your possessions. Take some time to consider all the areas of your life that need cleaning up.

Perhaps you might create smaller objectives for yourself, or perhaps you should assign additional tasks to family members and coworkers. In any case, the moment has come to process and remove anything excess. With any luck, these suggestions will enable you to organize your life and make a fresh start.

CHAPTER THREE

how-to-build-wealth

Many or all of the products featured here are from our partners who compensate us. This influences which products we write about and where and how the product appears on a page. However, this does not influence our evaluations. Our opinions are our own. Here is a list of our partners and here's how we make money.

The investing information provided on this page is for educational purposes only. NerdWallet does not offer advisory or brokerage services, nor does it recommend or advise investors to buy or sell particular stocks, securities or other investments.

How to build wealth in 5 steps

These five simple rules will help keep your retirement savings on track and growing for the long haul — and that means a Future You who's financially secure. Who doesn't like the sound of that?

1. Automate your savings

Life is busy. Maybe you noticed? That means you need to make sure you're contributing to your retirement account automatically. Because you know that any "must. do. this. now." task that suddenly stares you in the face — paying your credit card bill, watching that puppy video — is going to feel much more important in the moment than "saving money for some future date decades away."

You want your money quietly working for you in the background, no matter what's happening in your life or in the world. That's where automatic savings comes in. And hey, you've already nailed this with your 401(k). (Paycheck deductions, anyone?)

With a little work upfront, you can mimic that process with your IRA: Link your bank account to your IRA account and set up regularly scheduled transfers. (Some companies let employees automatically send money to their IRA from each paycheck. Ask your employer if that's a perk at your workplace.)

An added benefit to auto-saving plans is that you get to think less about your retirement account. Why is ignoring your account a good thing, you ask? Because when the market's tanking and your account balance is trending down, you don't want your hands anywhere near the "sell" button. Investing in stocks means riding out the tough times — and putting your savings on autopilot can make that easier. Incidentally, stock market crashes are a great time to distract yourself with a puppy video or two. (Seriously not kidding here. Here's more on what to do when the stock market crashes.)

2. Revisit your savings once a year

As we've been saying, when you're investing for a date far into the future, it's absolutely fine to let your money just sit there, quietly enjoying the highs (and surviving the lows) of the financial markets.

But it's also true that you probably shouldn't ignore your account entirely.

Here's why: Thanks to the market's gains and losses, your original asset allocation — how you divvied up your money among different types of stocks and bonds — will shift, and eventually get out of whack.

For example, say that when you opened your account, you decided to invest 70% in stocks and 30% in bonds. If the stock market has since increased in value, the proportion of your stock investments is going to grow; now maybe 80% of your holdings are in stocks.

Since bonds are a more conservative investment than stocks — they have less potential for growth, and less potential to plunge in value — your investment account would be riskier now compared with when you first created your retirement portfolio. If there were a stock market crash and your portfolio was 80% in stocks, rather than the 70% you'd originally chosen, you'd be in for an unpleasant surprise.

To reduce that risk, you need to rebalance, which means getting your investments back to the percentages you chose originally. (Now, if you're investing in a target-date fund, you don't need to rebalance — the fund manager will do it for you. And the same goes for many robo-advisors, which automatically rebalance your portfolio. That's one of the perks.)

One way to rebalance is to temporarily change how you're investing — for example, if your allocation to stocks has become too heavy, direct a larger portion of new account contributions to bonds for a bit. Slowly, as you invest more money, you'll shift the percentages you've invested in each asset class back to where you wanted them.

There are other ways to rebalance, too: We describe four methods in our guide to how to rebalance your retirement investments.

Financial experts have different opinions on how often you should rebalance. Generally, once a year is fine for a well-diversified investment portfolio. Pick a date and make it your rebalancing holiday, celebrated each year by spending a few minutes getting your investments back into balance. (Cake is optional, but encouraged.)

If all this talk of "asset allocation" and "rebalancing" is bringing on that overwhelmed feeling, that's understandable. Just breathe deep and remember there's a really easy way to get going on your retirement-savings goal: Hire a financial expert to help you.

That pro could be a low-cost robo-advisor — a company that uses technology to help make financial planning accessible. If that sounds appealing, take a look at our top picks for best robo-advisors. Or you could hire an actual human with whom you can talk things through. Check out our story on how to find the right financial advisor for you.

3. Hike your savings rate

Did we mention that it's awesome that you're saving for retirement? It's awesome. And you've already done the hardest part: getting started. The next step is easy: Hike up your savings rate a little bit every year.

It's easy because you can do it if and when your income rises. Say you get a raise or a bonus or some unexpected found money. Why not send just a little bit of that out to your future self? And if the year isn't great financially, you can always choose not to do it.

Small increases in your contribution rate can have an outsize effect on your future financial security. Check it out:

Remember how you need to visit your account once a year to rebalance? On that same date every year, see if you can't inch your savings rate just a little bit higher. Or, even easier: See if your 401(k) gives you the option to switch on annual auto-increases — if so, go flip that switch right now.

4. Avoid high fees

The same way that saving just a tiny bit more every year can push your retirement savings to lofty heights, seemingly small fees can have the opposite effect, taking a huge bite out of your account over your lifetime — you could lose more than $200,000 to fees in your 401(k) alone, according to a NerdWallet study.

So how do you make sure that money goes towards your retirement lifestyle, rather than to some random investment company? One solid way is to make sure you're investing in low-cost index mutual funds.

What counts as "low cost," you ask? A mutual fund with an expense ratio of 0.50% or less is a decent deal, though the best 401(k) plans offer mutual funds that charge less than 0.20%, which, obviously, is even better.

Fees are so important. Don't skip this! Maybe gather some friends and have a "cut the fees" party? You'd each log into your

IRA or 401(k) account, then click through to the summary page for each of your investments. The main fee to focus on is the expense ratio. Can you find a mutual fund with a similar investment objective, but a lower expense ratio? Just think: The money you save on investment costs will more than make up for the price of the wine you'll most definitely need to bribe people to come to this, um, party.

5. Stick with the market

With a goal like retirement, the stock market is your friend. That's not to say it can't be scary. It can be positively petrifying when the market tanks. And it will tank — it always does. But it always goes back up, too. If you're investing in a diversified portfolio — and of course you are! — then you're investing in thousands of companies in the

U.S. and abroad. To avoid the market is akin to saying: I think most companies worldwide are going to fail.

Rationally, we can agree that while many businesses do fail, many others thrive, and new companies are constantly emerging. When the market is tanking, it's no surprise that plenty of investors find themselves thinking this: "Well, I'll just get out of the stock market now, and get back in later, when things are looking up."

Trouble is, it's impossible to know when the market's going to turn around. And by exiting the market, even for a short time, you risk missing out on all kinds of gains.

So the next time the market falls, try this mantra on for size instead: "This is the best sale ever, and I don't even have to get up off the couch or click away from [enter name of whatever show you're currently binge-watching]. Thanks to those periodic transfers I'm making from my paycheck to my retirement accounts, I'm currently buying new mutual fund shares at a fraction of what they cost during the market's high point. When the market does turn around, as I know it will, I'm going to own way more shares than before, and they're all going to rise in value."

Building generational wealth

Remember, wealth isn't usually built over night, it takes time and consistency. This is especially true if your goal is to build generational wealth, which is when you pass assets down to future generations. You don't need tons of money to start building wealth, so even if you don't have much to start with, you can start where you are.

The more you contribute towards saving and investing and the sooner you start, the faster you should build wealth.

Also, don't be discouraged if you're just starting out, as long as you stick with it, compound interest will eventually work its magic.

CHAPTER FOUR

Methods for Saving Money and the Environment

Cutting Waste Through Meal Planning

Because you can plan out what you purchase, meal preparation is a terrific way to save money. You won't make as many impulsive purchases since you already have a list of the things you need to get. This reduces wasteful expenditure, which may significantly deplete your budget. You may order your groceries online so you won't make any impulsive purchases, and services like Instacart are becoming more popular.

It's beneficial to the environment, however. For instance, a third of all food is thought to end up in landfills. This implies that both the food and the effort, energy, and resources used to make it are wasted. We are squandering valuable resources when there is so much waste across so many industries.

But since you just purchase what you need when you meal prep, you may cut down on food waste. By doing this, you may reduce food waste and help save the resources used to produce the food.

Additionally, be careful to stay away from takeout. After a hard day at the office, it might be convenient to order takeout, but this is not the best option for the environment since takeout is expensive and served in disposable containers. It's a fantastic strategy to help control the need for takeout by preparing your meals ahead of time and bringing them with you to work.

Consume less meat

At first look, this appears a little disconnected from safeguarding the environment. But a pound of ground beef might require approximately or more than 1,800 gallons of water to create. As a nutritious, protein-rich plant-based substitute for ground beef, soybeans only need 200 gallons of water to produce one pound of them. As a result, eating vegetarian meals saves money over time since they use less water and other resources to produce.

Assume that a household of four consumes a pound of ground beef every time hamburgers are served. Even if they switch to a plant-based alternative only one day a week, they may save 100,000 gallons of water annually. The environmental effect is significant.

Additionally, if properly prepared, plant-based dinners are less expensive than meals that include meat. Consequently, you are protecting the environment and your cash at the same time.

Replace any items in your home that use energy.

Some of the most expensive home expenses are gas, electricity, and water, all of which affect the environment. For this reason, it's crucial to invest in cutting-edge technology that will help you save water and reduce your carbon impact. Although it may seem that doing this would cost you money rather than saving it, investing in cost-saving strategies for your home or yard will pay off in the long run.

The following are some of the most economical methods to improve your home while saving money:

Because it consumes less water, money is saved. And for the same reason, it's better for the environment.

This is essential if you have dripping faucets. Otherwise, all you're doing is squandering money on resources. And nobody benefits from it.

By conserving energy and bringing down your power bill, they help you save money. Additionally, compared to other lights, these bulbs last a lot longer and need less frequent replacement. Utilize natural illumination wherever possible to conserve money and power.

Numerous devices that use phantom power while they are off may be turned off using power strips. You may save money and release energy for use elsewhere on the grid by shutting off the electricity at the source.

This conserves water since flushing the toilet uses less water, and it's also free to install. As a result, you avoid purchasing to save money.

Spend money on reusable goods

Items that can be reused are another excellent purchase that will save you money and the environment. Because they lessen the total requirement for manufacture, reusable things are wonderful for the environment. It implies that by forgoing a single-use item, you are not only keeping it out of the garbage but also saving the massive quantities of energy required to produce it.

And moving to reusable things might help you save a lot of money. For instance, Americans spend billions annually on water bottles. You may save $260 a year by purchasing a reusable water bottle as opposed to purchasing one.

Other reusable items that can enable you to save money over time include:

Other reusable items that can enable you to save money over time include:

Glass Tupperware is recyclable and has a longer lifespan than plastic Tupperware.

You may save $50 a year by using cloth napkins rather than disposable ones.

Another great strategy to save costs is to use rags instead of paper towels since it eliminates a line item from your budget.

Despite being somewhat expensive, grocery bags prevent plastic from ending up in landfills.

Depending on the brand you choose to purchase, makeup apparel might save you $500.

Brushes made of bamboo are another good buy.

Another $200 a year may be saved by using reusable plastic bags.

When using your heating or cooling system, take into account

The fact that heating and air companies charge extra to operate their services during busy seasons is another intriguing scam. You can save a ton of money if you figure out when they are and choose to run during those times. Even some gas and electricity providers have unique programs you may enroll in to start saving money. Additionally, it lessens the total load on the grid during peak hours, which reduces energy consumption and conserves natural resources. A victory for the environment and one for you.

Regarding heating and cooling, you may want to think about adjusting your thermostat while you're not home. When you depart in the summer, raise the thermostat. Set it lower in the winter. For instance, if you typically keep your home at 68 degrees while you're at work in the summer, raise it to 72 degrees. By utilizing less power, money may be saved. When you arrive home, you can always put it back down. Even smart thermometers that you can set up to make these adjustments automatically exist.

Benefit from buying and selling used items

The growth of online flea markets has greatly improved our lives environmental impact. Finding or selling products has become easier and quicker thanks to websites like Facebook Marketplace, Craigslist, and others that facilitate resale. It's also fantastic for the environment. You're prolonging the life of a product that may have ended up in the garbage, and you're not paying for manufacturing methods that are bad for the environment.

You may sell any spare items you have laying around your home on Craigslist, Facebook Marketplace, or Poshmark, which is a great choice if you're trying to earn some money. Of course, it won't always be a reliable source of cash, but it aids in clutter removal, cost savings, and environmental protection.

You may even modernize outdated items to give them new life before using these internet discussion boards to sell your products. The future? It may develop into one of many successful side businesses!

Buy Nothing groups are a fantastic alternative to traditional retail outlets, and as an added

www.ingramcontent.com/pod-product-compliance
Lightning Source LLC
Chambersburg PA
CBHW070321220526
45465CB00013B/1977